Things Above

Elizabeth Krause

illustrated by

Christy Schneyman

*I dedicate this book to Jesus,
the relentless pursuer of my soul.
You gave Your all for me, even when
I wanted nothing to do with You.
I'm so grateful to be Yours.*

*In Love,
Elizabeth*

Therefore if you have been raised up with Christ, keep seeking the things above, where Christ is, seated at the right hand of God.

Set your mind on things above, not on the things that are on earth.

— **Colossians 3:1-2**

And His strong love

Oh, how He longs
to live with you there!

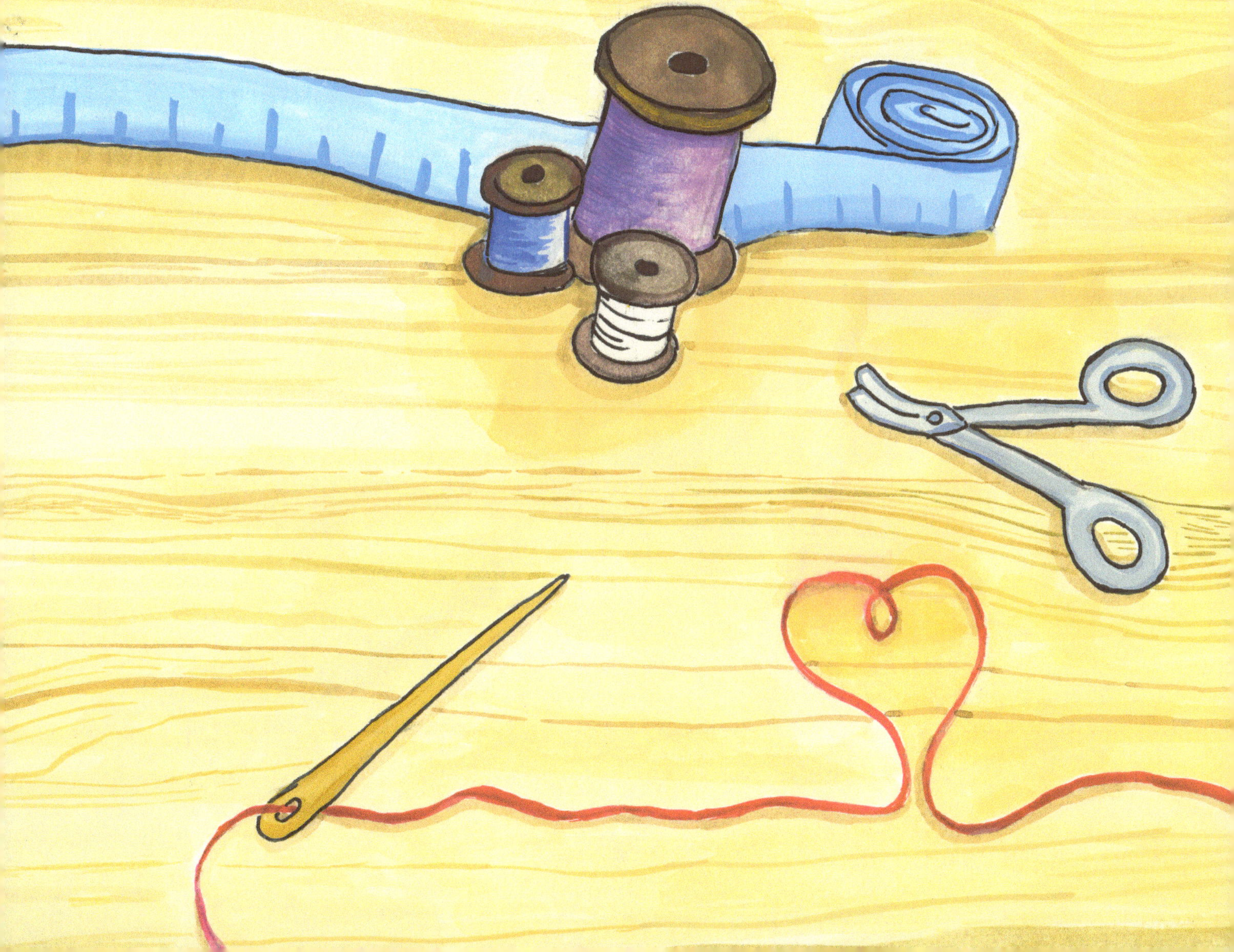

Won't you invite Him into your home?

The place in your heart most secret and deep

Give up the old to welcome His new

**Be His place of comfort,
Where He may lay His head.**

Set Your mind on Christ Jesus the King, and of His steadfast love daily sing.

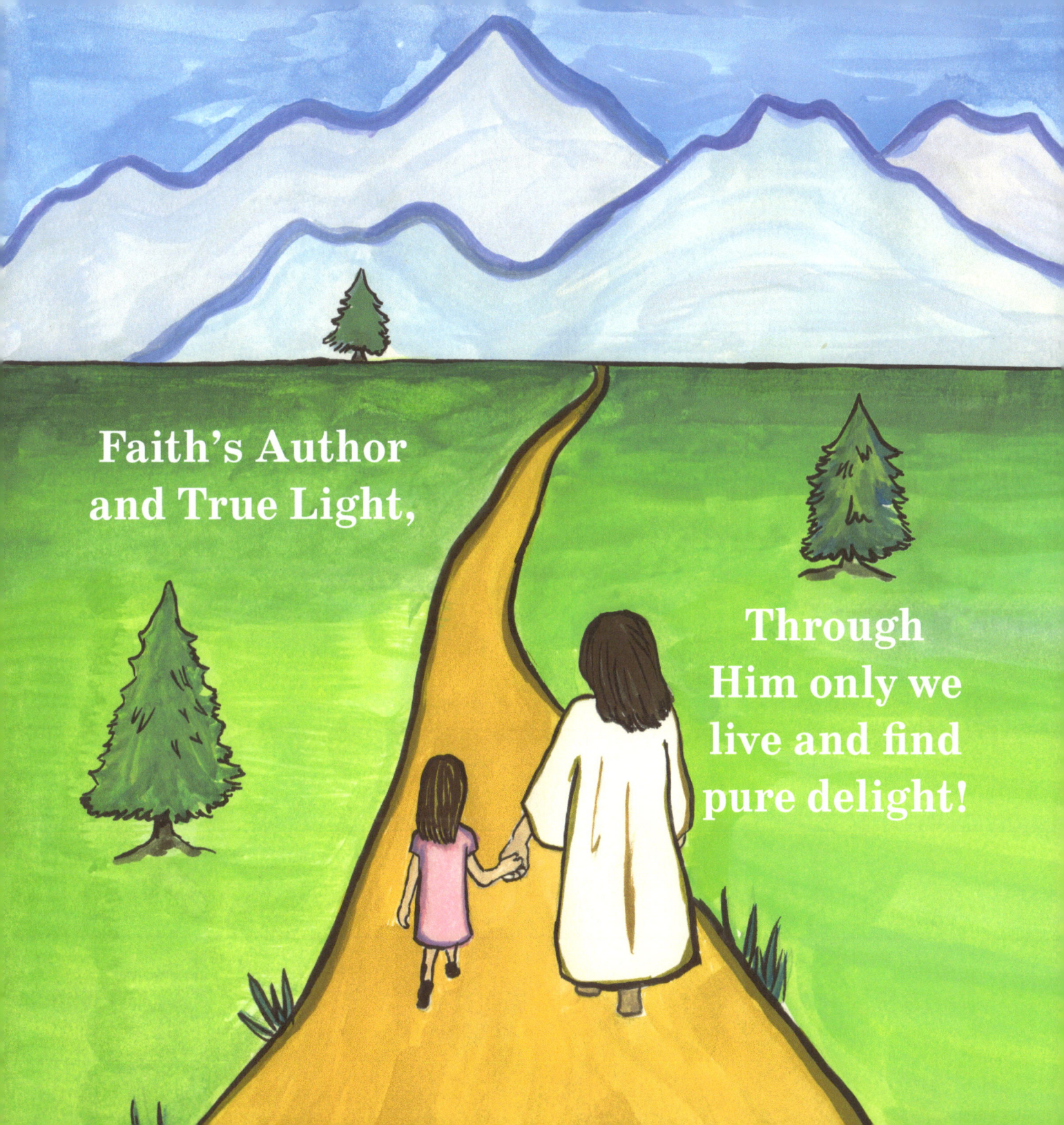

Author's Note

The image of heaven's throne room is an artistic interpretation and has been simplified for this children's story.

The throne room of heaven is a beautiful place! Ephesians 2:6 tells us that, when we believe in Jesus, we are seated with Him in heavenly places! Wow!

Take a look at these scriptures to see how the Bible describes the throne of God:

Jesus on the throne
Isaiah 6

A Heavenly Vision
Ezekiel 1

Jesus next to the Father
Colossians 3:1-3

Jesus in His glory
Revelation 4

Further Exploration for Parents and Kids

The Good News!

But some bad news first...

God created Heaven, the Universe, the Earth, and the people of Earth (including you and me). A loooong time ago, the very first man and woman that God created did not trust Him and disobeyed Him. As a result, sin and death entered our world. Sin has darkened everything on the Earth—even us.[1]

The Bible tells us that everyone has sinned and fallen short of the glory of God. Sin is disobedience to God, and it brings death. We have all disobeyed God by going our own way. We've said, done, or believed things that are not a part of God's perfect, loving, and holy nature. Sin separates us from being with God and hurts His heart. The Bible says that even the good deeds we do without God are really just dirty rags. There is nothing we can do by ourselves to find closeness with Him. We need a Savior!

But wait!

God *wants* us to know Him—like, REALLY *know* Him (like a brother or a best friend)! He wants to be with us *so much* that He did what we could not do by ourselves.[2]

God loved us in this way: He sent Jesus, His SON, to save us so that we can know Him! This is eternal life![3]

Jesus came to Earth, lived a perfect life with NO SIN, and died on the cross for *our* sins. He suffered the death that we were doomed to die; and three days later, He came back to life!

Jesus paid the debt that we owed. This means that when we turn to Him, and away from sin, we are forgiven and set free from sin. We become God's children![4]

Thank You, Jesus, our Perfect Savior![5]

After He came back to life, Jesus went up, up, up... through the clouds to Heaven, and He sat down on a big beautiful throne next to the Father. He is coming back here soon to be with us forever.[6]

Don't worry, though!

He did not leave us all by ourselves! He sent His Holy Spirit to us. This means that when we make Jesus our Lord, His Holy Spirit comes to live in our hearts forever![7]

---

1. Genesis 1-3
2. Romans 8:3
3. John 3:16-17, John 17:3
4. 1 Peter 2:21-22, Ephesians 2:4-6
5. John 1:29
6. Acts 1:9, 1 Thessalonians 4:16-17, John 14:3
7. John 14:16, John 16:7,13-14

Do You Want to Follow Jesus?

Deciding to follow Jesus is a BIG decision.

It means to turn away from our old life of sin—disobeying God and doing things our own way—and follow Him as His children! We give up our own lives and follow Jesus. Jesus helps us with His grace. If He asks us to do something that we can't do by ourselves, He gives us the ability (or grace) to do it. We just have to come to Him![8]

Life with Jesus is a great adventure AND it will not always be easy.

Many people will be excited about your decision! But others may not understand. They may even be unkind when they see your love for Jesus because they do not know Him yet.[9]

Take courage!

There is no reason to be afraid when you know Jesus.

Whether things in life seem very easy or very hard, we get to run to our kind, strong, loving Father in every moment. That is where we find peace. He is a BIG God. He is our Faithful Fortress, and He comforts us with His love.[10]

The Bible says that "if you confess (say) with your mouth, 'Jesus is Lord,' and believe in your heart that God raised Him from the dead, you will be saved."[11]

We come close to God through accepting Jesus as His free gift to us.[12]

If you want to meet Jesus, you can start with this simple prayer:

"Dear Jesus. I have sinned against You. I have hurt Your heart by disobeying You and doing things my own way. Please forgive me! I believe that You are God, and I give You my life. I belong to You now. I believe that You died for my sins and came back to life so that I could be with You! I give You my life. I choose to follow You. Please fill me with Your Holy Spirit. Thank You that You have forgiven me! Thank You that You have adopted me; that You have made me Your child. Thank You that You love me so very much, and I am a part of Your FAMILY now!"[13]

Yay! Let's celebrate! The Bible tells us that ALL of heaven throws a party when you give your life to Jesus.[14] He is so excited and so happy! You *are* His child.

---

8   Matthew 4:19, Matthew 16:24
9   Matthew 5:10-12
10 Matthew 11:28-30, Hebrews 10:19-23, Psalm 91:4, Zephaniah 3:17
11 Romans 10:9
12 John 10:9, John 14:6, Ephesians 2:8-9
13 Romans 12:4-5, Ephesians 2:19-22
14 Luke 15:7,10

Growing in Love

Our friendship with Jesus does not stop with one prayer. Friendship with Him is meant to grow! Here are some things we get to do with Jesus as His friends:

Pray – Prayer is conversation with God. This conversation never has to stop! Even though we can talk to Him in every moment, Jesus says it is important to spend time alone with God.

Jesus tells us to "pray to our Father who is in secret," and Father God will hear us! Find a time and a place where you can be with Him—no distractions. God has something new for us every day, but we have to come to Him to get it! It's like getting fresh baked bread straight from heaven's bakery every morning! His daily bread makes us stronger!

When you pray, Jesus's Holy Spirit is right there with you. He will teach you to pray, just ask Him! The Bible gives us many examples of how to pray. Matthew 6:9-13 is a great place to start. Talk to Him out loud. He sees everything, so you do not have to hide anything from Him. Sing Him a song—praise Him and dance with Him. Ask to see His face. Ask Him what He is thinking. Be still and listen!

Be sure to have your Bible, a notebook, and a pencil handy. You'll be surprised at all the wonderful things He wants to share with you.[15]

Read the Bible – God wrote us a letter. It's called the Bible! It's very special to Him. It's about His Son, and it is full of precious gems! We get to hide this treasure safely inside of our hearts.[16] We can read it, sing its words, and write about it! We get to read this book with the Author (God's Holy Spirit), and God uses His word to heal our minds, hearts, and bodies.[17] If you are still learning to read, ask your parents, older siblings, or a trusted adult to read the Bible to you every day! His word gives us life.

Get Baptized in Water – Baptism is when we get dunked in water to bury our old life of sin. We go into the water with the Holy Spirit and come out squeaky clean! Now, nothing of the old life can stick to us.[18] If you've met Jesus, talk to a parent, pastor, or trusted adult who loves Jesus, too, and ask them to baptize you in water.

Get Baptized in the Holy Spirit - Just as we get dunked in water, Jesus wants us dunked in His Holy Spirit! The Bible says Jesus will plunge us into the depths of His Spirit so that we can boldly do what He did while He was on Earth . . . and even greater works! This means we get to follow the Holy Spirit's lead to bravely tell others about Jesus; He wants to set captives free, heal broken hearts, help the blind see, feed the hungry, and more. He wants to do these things with us! We are His hands and

---

15 Luke 10:42, Romans 8:26, Psalm 27:8, Philippians 4:6, Matthew 6:6, Matthew 6:9-13, 1 Thessalonians 5:16-18, Matthew 18:19-20
16 Psalm 119:11, Deuteronomy 11:18
17 Ephesians 5:26, Hebrews 4:12, Psalm 107:20
18 Acts 22:16, John 3:5, Romans 6:3-4

feet. Ask Jesus to baptize you with His Spirit.[19] The Holy Spirit is God. He always points to Jesus as Lord, and always agrees with the Bible.[20]

Find a Church – God has adopted us into His family! This means we were made to walk together with other people who know Jesus. We come together to love Jesus and grow in love for one another.[21]

Forgiveness – With His help, we get to take the forgiveness God gives us and offer it to others.[22] We find freedom in accepting and giving the forgiveness of Jesus.

Tell others about Jesus – We get to share the gift of Jesus's love with the people around us! We can tell them what Jesus did for us and how knowing Him is the reason we are alive![23]

19	Matthew 3:11, Luke 3:16, John 1:33
20	1 John 4:1
21	Romans 12:4-6, Romans 12:9-16, Hebrews 10:24-25
22	Matthew 6:12,14-15
23	Matthew 28:19

About the Author

Elizabeth Krause is a child of God and really just a child at heart. Through her writing, Elizabeth hopes to provoke young (and not-so-young) readers to a lifestyle of searching out the inexhaustible beauty and wonder of Jesus and His Gospel. A Texas native with a background in kids ministry, Elizabeth enjoys devouring the Word of God, sharing the love of Jesus with others, exploring nature, cooking with her family, and dabbling in various creative arts.

About the Illustrator

With a Bachelor's in Illustration and a Master's in Art Teaching, Christy Schneyman has a passion for revealing God's creativity through painting and visual arts. Her primary mediums are watercolor and gouache. An educator at heart, Christy hopes to inspire young creatives in their own artistic expression and connection with the Creator Himself.

Things Above
Published by Dauntless Pursuit
Text Copyright © 2024 by Elizabeth Krause
Illustrations Copyright © 2024 by Christy Schneyman

All rights reserved. No part of this book may be reproduced, stored in a retrieval system, or transmitted, in any form or by any means without the prior written permission of the publisher, nor be otherwise circulated in any form of binding or cover other than that in which it is published and without a similar condition being imposed on the subsequent purchaser.

Scripture taken from the NEW AMERICAN STANDARD BIBLE®, Copyright ©1995 by The Lockman Foundation. Used by permission.

ISBN 13 TP: 979-8-218-55750-8
ISBN 13 HC: 979-8-218-55749-2

For Worldwide Distribution

www.ingramcontent.com/pod-product-compliance
Lightning Source LLC
LaVergne TN
LVHW072058070426
835508LV00002B/165